A Shark in a Fish Tank

15 Principles of Intrapreneurship

Jordan Levitt

Contents

Introduction:

What is an Intrapreneur?

Intrapreneurship is a type of system that allows employees to act like entrepreneurs within their organization or company. The great thing about intrapreneurs is that they are proactive, action-oriented, and self-motivated individuals who always take the initiative instead of waiting to be told what to do.

In an intrapreneurship, employees are given an opportunity to utilize their entrepreneurial skills thus, creating an entrepreneurial environment. This type of environment also gives freedom to the employees to grow and experiment within their organization.

Intrapreneurs have the ability to solve issues such as cutting costs or increasing productivity. They are able to think outside of the box and lead others when they're given a task or assignment. Also, intrapreneurs aren't afraid to take risks when they know that their actions will benefit the organization. If you're wondering whether you have the potential to become an intrapreneur, here is a quick rundown of traits or characteristic intrapreneurs possess:

- They're proud, competitive, and they love to be the best.
- They enjoy improving until they become the best at what they do.
- They don't appreciate rules or being told what to do.
- They don't appreciate being boxed in, they crave freedom.
- They are an incredible asset to any company.
- They want to be able to make enough money, so they don't have to think about making money.
- They have the ability to motivate other people around them.

Successful intrapreneurs feel comfortable enough to test their own ideas until they achieve the results they desire. They're also able to visualize and interpret market trends to ensure that their organization stays ahead of the competition. With all these traits, who wouldn't want to become an intrapreneur?

Intrapreneur vs. Entrepreneur
The first time the term "intrapreneur" appeared was back in the 1980s when Elizabeth and Gifford Pinchot, a couple of management consultants published the book entitled *Intrapreneuring: Why You Don't Have to Leave the*

Corporation to Become an Entrepreneur. In the book, intrapreneurs were defined as dreamers who take action, those who create innovation within their business.

Although this term has been around for some time now, some people still get confused between intrapreneurship and entrepreneurship. The main difference between intrapreneurs and entrepreneurs is that intrapreneurs are within entrepreneurs or they are entrepreneurs within large organizations who utilize entrepreneurial skills without having to deal with the risks that come with such activities.

Most of the time, intrapreneurs have the ability to work on projects within their organization which foster innovation. On the other hand, entrepreneurs are people who, instead of working as employees for organizations or businesses, they run their own businesses. Therefore, they have to deal with both the rewards and risks of the business they have started on their own. As different as these two types of individuals are, they do share some key traits:

- **Leadership:** Both intrapreneurs and entrepreneurs possess strong leadership skills, which they need to motivate others to achieve a single goal.
- **Vision and intelligence:** They both have the ability to recognize trends, capitalize on emerging opportunities, and they possess the required tools and skill sets to complete different kinds of projects.
- **Adaptability:** They have the ability to change direction as needed whenever challenges or problems arise.

Both intrapreneurs and entrepreneurs are amazing assets to any company. Later on, we will be discussing how they can work together and help each other for the benefit of their organizations.

Intrapreneur vs. Employee

As much as employers would like all of their employees to think creatively and have the initiative to seize each opportunity that comes along, this isn't always the case. Not all employees have out-of-the-box thinking as part of their skill set. Therefore, employers must be able to differentiate employees from intrapreneurs within their organization.

Employees are individuals who perform all their duties and responsibilities, which are part of their own job descriptions. They focus on succeeding at their current role within their company instead of focusing on upward advancement or on the overall success of the organization. Because of this, employees have the tendency to quickly shift from their current job to another if they're offered higher pay. They don't really think about their future within the same company as they focus more on their own career.

Conversely, intrapreneurs are those who create for themselves a job description which is more robust and a lot broader. They have no problem with embracing the caveats at the end of most job descriptions which read "other duties as assigned" or something else to that effect. Instead of just fulfilling their own duties and responsibilities, they also focus on finding new ways to grow within the company and to help the company grow as well. Most of the time, intrapreneurs stay with their company long-term in order to help improve the business. They know that when the profits of the company increase, they will be rewarded by receiving higher pay. In other words, they are big-picture thinkers who know how to envision a better future and work hard to achieve it.

PART 1:
WHO YOU ARE

Chapter 1:

First off,
Are You an Intrapreneur?

Any organization, business or corporation requires a strong core team. For the business to grow, develop, and succeed, having a core team of intrapreneurs or entrepreneurs within the organization would be highly beneficial. In order to become an intrapreneur, you must work independently within your company to diversify and revitalize by introducing innovation.

As an intrapreneur, you would try to come up with solutions for problems which are either under or beyond your control. You don't just stop by thinking out-of-the-box. Instead, you make those ideas you come up with a reality. Unlike other employees in the organization, you're always able to rise up to the occasion and save the day. Here are some things, which make you an intrapreneur:

- **You believe in the mission and vision of your company and you have faith in its potential for growth**

  Simply working for a startup business in order to earn a monthly income doesn't make you an intrapreneur. You must genuinely believe in the mission and vision of your company as well as in its potential to keep on growing. You're hopeful, courageous, and optimistic enough to overcome your vices and embrace your values.

- **You're an important part of your company's core team**

  As an intrapreneur of your organization, you will keep on contributing to its growth and success. You will be doing such an amazing job that you become a vital part of your company's core team. You don't just work because you have to. You have a powerful sense of responsibility and genuine concern whenever you make decisions because you know that these decisions have a direct effect on the growth of your organization.

- **You're extremely resourceful and have the ability to perform high-end multitasking**

  You make use of all of the available resources wisely that you're able to accomplish your task even if you don't have everything you need. You identify problems as they arise and are able to quickly think of and employ solutions. Being an intrapreneur also means that you know how to coordinate with other people and other teams in such a way that you become part of them. This also makes you accountable for the responsibilities of the people you work with.

- **You're not afraid to take risks in your career**
  Intrapreneurs aren't afraid to take risks. No matter how big the risk might seem, if you think it's worth taking, you'll push through with it. For instance, if big companies ask you to join them and entice you with more money, you would first look at the big picture.

  You think about the future you have in your current company and how you can help it grow (remember, intrapreneurs are genuinely concerned with the company), and make a choice to turn down the job offer because you can see yourself succeeding along with your company in the near future. You're not just concerned with yourself; you also think about the journey you are on along with the people in the company you've invested all your time in. You're able to achieve both your goals and the goals of your company.

- **You want to expand and spread a culture of intrapreneurship in the organization**
  Intrapreneurs also aim to spread their culture throughout the organization. Once you've learned how to

become a successful intrapreneur, you would also like the other people to follow suit. To do this, you would share your knowledge with them and encourage them to do the same. If you're able to spread this type of culture, you'll start seeing the positive impact it will have in your organization.

Characteristics of Intrapreneurs

Intrapreneurs are an important asset of any organization. They're able to apply the required entrepreneurship principles to any task assigned to them. As long as you have intrapreneurs within your organization, you'll be on your way to growth and success! If you want to become one, then you must have the required characteristics. Here are some of the best characteristics of intrapreneurs:

- **Problem-solvers**

  This is one of the most standout traits of intrapreneurs. If you want to become an intrapreneur, you must have excellent problem-solving skills. But if you want to hire intrapreneurs for your company, choose those who you know are able to solve different kinds of problems no matter what the situation is.

- **Self-starters**

  Intrapreneurs are also superb self-starters. Just because you are part of an organization, this doesn't mean that you can't be a self-starter. You must be able to keep yourself motivated, so you can always be better than you were the day before. This is one of the best ways for you to grow. Motivation is a huge part of being a self-starter as it pushes you to transform from a passive participant into an active leader.

Intrapreneurs have a good idea of what their purpose in life is. They always know what they need to do each day and they always have the initiative to perform beyond what is expected of them. If you're in charge of hiring new employees, make sure to look out for such people.

- **Innovative**

  The next thing you must learn if you want to become an intrapreneur is how to be innovative. You should be able to provide innovative solutions to problems, but you should also be able to nurture the best ideas. When you hear an idea from another person and it makes you feel intrigued, you'll keep on thinking about it until you find a way to make that idea a reality.

- **Growth-drivers**

  If you love growth and you love pushing yourself to become the best at what you do, then you have the potential to become a great intrapreneur. Don't wait for other people to tell you how or when it's time to grow.

Keep making plans until you're able to succeed at achieving your goals. Even if you run into challenges, you don't have to give up. Change your course and this will help propel your growth.

- **Integrity**
Intrapreneurs are both humble and confident. Aside from this, you should also have your own sense of purpose and superb self-awareness. With these characteristics, intrapreneurs are able to stick to their own principles and values making it easier for them to focus on what's important.

- **They don't measure their success by the money they earn**
This doesn't mean that intrapreneurs don't respect the importance and value of money. However, they do understand the economic drivers which propel the organization to success. They support and accept with fundamental truth instead of fighting it. While employees only see the value of their work through the money they earn, intrapreneurs look beyond that, so they're able to put all their effort into the work they do.

- **"Greenhousers"**
This means that intrapreneurs are always trying to find ways to nurture ideas (the good ones), and make them

grow. To them, ideas are seeds which need the proper care and all the other factors to make them grow. If you want to become a great intrapreneur, you must learn to keep on finding ways to turn ideas into real and actionable plans.

- **Authentic**

  Finally, intrapreneurs are genuine. You can't fake being an intrapreneur. Unless you learn these characteristics and apply them to your life, you can't become a true intrapreneur. The good news is that you can learn how to become this type of person no matter who you are or where you are in your life right now. As long as you have the drive and the willingness to learn, it's never too late to make this positive change in your life.

Chapter 2:

Identify, Analyze, and Polish Your Best Skills and Assets

If you want to become an intrapreneur, this doesn't just mean that you try to become a constructive team member in the organization. You need to have certain characteristics and a willingness to see yourself and your organization achieve your goals. You need to be able to bring something to your business that nobody else in the organization can. As an intrapreneur, you need to share your mind, your vision, your voice, and your story to your organization.

Before you start working towards becoming an intrapreneur, you need to learn more about yourself. You need to be able to identify, analyze, and polish all of your best skills and assets. As an intrapreneur, you should give your company all the best parts of yourself in order to thrive and help your company grow. Growth is an important part of the process and unless you learn all that you can about yourself, you won't be able to truly give your all.

Have you ever thought about the trending things in the world now? Game consoles, social media platforms, and even ingenious inventions which are being used all over the world. All of these iconic things were created by the best intrapreneurs within the organizations and companies they came from. These are the products of those who act and think like entrepreneurs while they work for a bigger company.

As an intrapreneur, you need to use all of your assets and skills to take the initiative to create amazing new ideas, products, policies, processes, and more for your company while still following its objectives, values, and mission. Being an intrapreneur doesn't mean being a rebel. It simply means that you should have the desire and courage to go after any idea which you believe will be beneficial to your customers, your clients, and your company.

What are Your Best Skills and Assets?

In order to work on to improve your best skills and assets, you must first identify them. If this is your first time to even consider this concept, then you may have to take a moment of reflection to discover more about yourself.

After making the decision to become an invaluable intrapreneur in your organization, take some time to sit down and think about what you're really good at. Make a list of all your skills and assets. Don't leave anything out. Think about instances at work when you know you did really well. Then think about the skills you used during these instances which helped you accomplish your task or achieve your goal.

Now try to see which of those skills and assets are aligned with the core values and strategies. Also, try to come up with some ideas which you think can help your company grow and move forward. Now, how do you think you can make these ideas of yours a reality? By applying your best skills and assets, of course!

If you want your superiors to accept and support your journey towards intrapreneurship, you must give them a reason to do so. Let them know about these skills you have and how you can uniquely influence your organization in the best possible way. The first step you must take to do this is to identify what your most exceptional skills and assets are.

Everyone is good at something. The only problem with most employees is that they aren't willing to apply their skills for the sake of their organization. Most employees only look out for themselves, which is why they have no problem moving from one organization to another even after investing so much time and effort in the company they are already in. Unless you commit to the growth and success of your company, you won't have the desire to apply these skills even after you've identified them. Of course, after you've identified these skills, it's time to start improving them. Only then will you be able to apply these skills in order to become the best intrapeneur you can be.

Analyzing and Polishing Your Best Skills and Assets

Now that you've identified your best skills and assets, it's time to start analyzing and polishing them. Doing this helps you become a better intrapreneur. Here are some tips to help you out:

- **Don't be afraid to work on your personal skills**

  Intrapreneurs share a lot of the same skills, assets, and strengths as entrepreneurs. As aforementioned, the difference is that intrapreneurs work within a bigger organization while entrepreneurs start their own businesses. As an intrapreneur, you must develop your creativity and self-confidence while learning how to be a tenacious innovator. Learn how to solve problems and don't be afraid of sharing your ideas with other people.

  As an intrapreneur, you shouldn't be afraid of taking calculated risks. This doesn't mean that you should just take risks willy-nilly. You must learn how to differentiate bad risks from good ones so you can decide which types of risks you should take. Also, keep in mind that success won't always happen. Therefore, you must also be brave enough to pursue your ideas even though you know that failure is always a possibility. Each time you're faced with a challenge, learn how to make use of your skills to overcome it and come out on top.

- **Come up with an idea**

  Intrapreneurs are the type of people who would always look for ways to improve current situations. If you see or experience any problems, look at them as opportunities in disguise. This is another way you can polish your best skills.

Right now, try to come up with an idea to solve a specific issue your company is facing. Be as specific as possible and when you're trying to come up with the idea, make sure it involves all of the skills you're good at. This requires you to analyze your skills and think about how you can use them for the benefit of your company. Try to think of a really amazing idea which has a high chance of making a positive impact on the problem you're trying to solve.

- **Share your idea with others**
After you've thought of your idea and formulated a plan of action, it's time to share it with other people. Of course, you can only make a difference in your organization if you share this idea to the right people. Talk to your superiors about your idea and tell them how you can contribute by applying your best skills and assets.

The best way to improve these skills is by applying and practicing them in real-life situations. The more you're able to apply your skills, the better they will become. Then you can start thinking about other skills which you can polish by repeating this process all over again.

- **Learn how to think on your feet**

  As a bonus tip, learning how to think on your feet can also help you improve your skills. As long as you know what you're good at and what you're able to do, you can always apply these skills whenever the need arises.

  Be aware of everything which happens in your organization. Whether you're in the process of executing a plan of action or you're just dealing with your day-to-day tasks, you must be ready to think on your feet. When an issue comes up, try to think of a solution and how you can help make things better. This will definitely work to your advantage as you're trying to learn how to be a highly skilled intrapreneur.

Chapter 3:

Determine the Kind of Growth That Best Suits You

Although intrapreneurs and entrepreneurs differ from one another, this doesn't mean that they don't have anything in common. Although entrepreneurs work in their own capacity and intrapreneurs have the resources of their organization at their disposal, they both have the drive and passion to take calculated risks and innovate. If you know that you have the qualities of a great entrepreneur but you're still waiting for the right opportunity to come along, you may first want to start as an intrapreneur. Use your passion and skills to search for opportunities to improve your business.

For intrapreneurs, their growth never stops. They continue growing along with the company they are trying to improve. Before we go into the different kinds of growth and how to determine which type is right for you, here are some tips to keep in mind:

- **There's no need to be shy**

  If you work hard, you respect your company and everyone in it, and if you have a steadfast drive, then you already have the makings of a great intrapreneur. The same thing goes if you're innately innovative and you aren't afraid to take risks after you've considered them. There's no need to be shy, it's alright to label yourself as an intrapreneur. Be confident enough but just don't get cocky and keep on trying to prove yourself to your company and to those you work with.

- **Help out but try not to be pushy**

  If you see others struggling with their tasks or responsibilities, approach them by trying to be helpful instead of being imposing or authoritative. It's always important to treat everyone with respect no matter what their position is in the organization. Remember that overall, your goal as an intrapreneur is to support your company and not to take over others.

- **Recognize and take responsibility**

  Finally, you should remember that you have an excellent chance to create a lasting impact on the success of your company as an intrapreneur. Showcase the skills you have developed to show that you're an invaluable asset to the company and not just another employee who would have no problem taking a new job when offered higher pay.

As an intrapreneur, you must recognize that it's your responsibility to work towards being a great employee each and every day. Make your company known through social media, get involved with events hosted by your company, talk about your company whenever the opportunity arises, and so on. As small as these tasks may seem, when you keep doing them, they will leave a lasting impression on those you interact with which, in turn, makes your company more well known and established.

Different Kinds of Growth

Anyone who works in a company aims to build a career and a professional future. As soon as you are hired, you start thinking about the growth and development of your career within the company which hired you. This would involve you changing positions as your skills improve and as you gain more experience through the work you do. But when it comes to your career, do you know that there are different kinds of growth?

First, there's a horizontal type of career growth. Here, you would get transferred to another department, so that you can have new experiences and learn new things. Through this kind of growth, you can also apply the skills you've been trying to develop and improve. Usually, those who are transferred to other departments hold the same status as they did in their previous department.

Then there's a vertical type of career growth. Here, you would be climbing the corporate ladder in your own department. Your goal for this type of growth is to end up becoming the leader of the department you're in right now. If you haven't even thought about the kind of career growth you prefer as you become an intrapreneur, here are the advantages and disadvantages of each:

- **Horizontal growth**

  The first advantage of this kind of career growth is that you can challenge yourself professionally and learn new things in the process. This would be a great option if you think that you won't have any chance to grow professionally within your department. Also, you will get the chance to meet and interact with new people while learning interesting things along the way. Horizontal growth also allows you to experience a new way of solving problems and thinking. Through this kind of growth, you can also try out a new kind of leadership approach.

  One of the biggest disadvantages of this kind of growth is that the salary you might receive from the position can either be the same or even smaller than the salary you are receiving in your current position. Of course, you would have to adjust to the new responsibilities while you're learning the ins and outs of the new department. If you're not a fan of change (which means you might not be ready to become an intrapreneur yet), then this kind of career growth isn't ideal for you. Also, you may want to consider the fact that working in a different department might not be as enjoyable or fulfilling for you.

- **Vertical growth**
  For this kind of growth, the biggest advantage is that you will be able to gain all the experiences in your department until you can call yourself an expert. Since you need a specific set of skills to work in the current department you're in, you can keep on improving these skills. It's easier to visualize your progress as well, especially if you're given promotions within your department. Change isn't as challenging in vertical growth and it usually comes with financial benefits. Also, changing positions won't be as uncomfortable because you'd still be working in the same department with the same set of coworkers.

  Of course, the main disadvantage of this kind of career growth is that you might start getting bored with it, especially if the tasks each member of the department does is fairly similar. Even if you're promoted, you would be doing the same things over and over again, each and every day. For this kind of growth, you might not be able to challenge yourself, especially if you aren't keen on becoming an intrapreneur. But if you are, then you will still be able to look for ways to improve your department for the benefit of your company. However, if you were able to reach the top of your department, you might start wondering what comes next.

As you can see, both kinds of professional growth come with their own pros and cons. Now it's up to you to decide which kind you're comfortable with. As you learn how to become an intrapreneur, you must also decide how you want your future in the company to be. This way, you can plan more effectively and come up with the best possible strategies.

Determining Which Suits Your Own Personality

The kind of growth you choose for yourself would depend on your own personality. Although some employees have no choice but to go where their superiors send them, this doesn't have to be the case for you, especially after you've proven your worth and value as an intrapreneur in your company.

Don't be afraid to communicate with your employers regarding your plans for growth within the organization. Most of the time, employers would appreciate such a conversation because they know that you want to keep working with them for the foreseeable future. Also, thinking about the growth you'd like to have in the company shows them how loyal you are and how much you want to work towards achieving the goals of the company along with them.

Think about all of the pros and cons of both horizontal

and vertical growth. Then think about your own skills and how you want to apply them to your work. Finally, think about how either kind of growth would benefit you personally and how each of them would help you on your journey towards becoming an intrapreneur. After considering all of these factors, you will be able to make a more informed decision about the kind of growth you should take within your organization.

Chapter 4:

Identify Your Interest and Needs?

Have you ever thought about where you are in your career right now? We've defined intrapreneurship, entrepreneurship, and being an employee. Most people in companies are employees. In fact, you may be classified as an employee right now. Even if you possess some of the qualities of entrepreneurs or intrapreneurs, you might still be a simple employee in your company right now.

Of course, there is nothing wrong with this. However, if you want to improve yourself and your whole organization, there's no better time than the present to start your journey towards becoming an intrapreneur. The next step to take is to think about your own interests and the needs you would like to fulfill in your life.

If you really want to become invested in your work, you must find it fulfilling. You must be interested in what you're doing, and you must find fulfillment in it. If you're able to achieve both of these through intrapreneurship, the whole process becomes a lot easier for you. The best part is, your needs and interests are part of you. So, with a little bit of self-examination, you will be able to find the answer to these questions.

Identifying Your Interests

You'd think it would be easy to think about what interests you. But when it comes to your job and applying your interests to intrapreneurship, sometimes you may find this step challenging. But this doesn't always have to be the case. For instance, you work in a manufacturing company. For such a company, you already manufacture specific products for the general public.

In such a situation, you may try thinking about your own interests. Let's say your company produces beach apparel and one of your interests is surfing. You can use this to come up with an idea of an entire surfing line your company can produce. This doesn't mean that you should go right up to your boss and tell him that you have a brilliant idea for a surfing line.

After identifying your interests, make sure to integrate and incorporate these into your company. You must think of ways to make these interests relevant to your company. Otherwise, your boss might think you're just wasting their time. Remember, you want to make the best impression, so your superiors would see you as a valuable intrapreneur instead of an employee with "wacky ideas." Here are some ways you can start applying intrapreneurship after you've thought about and identified your interests, which are compatible with your company:

- **Be proactive**

  After identifying your interests and thinking of ways to apply them to your company, it's time to start planning. Why waste the time you spent thinking, by simply putting your ideas on the shelf? Take the initiative by coming up with plans to implement your ideas before approaching your bosses.

- **Think about the questions which might be asked of you**

  Before approaching your superiors with your ideas, try to think of all the questions they might ask you. This will make you more prepared to answer such questions in a calm and intelligent way.

- **Be prepared to make quick adjustments as needed**

  Even if you're able to successfully incorporate your interests into your plans and you're already in the process of executing those plans, you must always be prepared for any changes. You must be open and flexible so that you can re-focus on your priorities when the situation calls for it.

- **Challenge the norm**

  If you have found a way to solve problems or make

things better in the organization, do something about it. You may ask permission from your superiors if you think it's needed, but as long as the change is within your control, don't be afraid to initiate it. If the change involves something you're interested in, all the better!

- **Document all of your accomplishments**

  Finally, it's always useful to document your accomplishments for future reference. For instance, you've made a plan or suggestion and you were given the go-signal to push through with it. If you managed to successfully implement your plan and it had a significant positive impact on the company, add this to your portfolio.

  This is what intrapreneurs do. They keep moving forward and adding new experiences to their portfolios. In doing this, you will never forget the things you've done and all the accomplishments you've had. This can serve as your motivation, your reference, and you can also use it to come up with new ideas for the things you're interested in.

How to Fulfill Your Needs

Intrapreneurs are always trying to create, innovate, and solve problems. They think outside of the box and they're willing to take risks after they've considered the whole situation. They inspire, lead, and they genuinely want to see their company grow along with them.

But if you want to continue becoming an intrapreneur within your company, you must also know how to fulfill your own needs. When you work to help your organization improve and grow, this must give you a sense of fulfillment. Otherwise, you might end up losing interest in what you're doing. If you're able to do work that's both interesting and fulfilling to you, you will keep doing it with no signs of stopping.

But how can you do this? How can you fulfill your needs while you're also trying to become an intrapreneur? Here are a couple of questions you may want to ask yourself in order for you to follow the right path:

- **Will you be able to handle the financial risk?**

  Most of the time, projects, plans or decisions made within an organization may come with financial risk. No matter how small your plan is, you must assess the financial risk first. As an intrapreneur, you should also think about this aspect the same way as an entrepreneur would. After all, an intrapreneur is simply an entrepreneur who works within an organization.

  If you're able to answer this question confidently, then you may continue with the task you have planned. And if you're able to achieve this plan, it would come with a sense of fulfillment as you know that you were able to help your company improve in a significant way.

- **What is your purpose?**

  As an intrapreneur, you are intrinsically motivated to always do your best no matter what the situation is. You're not motivated by money nor are you doing the work for the sake of recognition. In order to feel fulfilled with what you're doing, you must know what your purpose is.

  Think about what motivates you and why you want to become an intrapreneur in the first place. Do you want to make a significant impact on your company or on your society? Do you want to see your plans, vision or ideas come to life? Do you want your company to grow and succeed to benefit everyone in it including you? When you know your purpose, you know why you work, why you plan, and why you keep trying to improve yourself. And each time you're able to accomplish something, you will definitely feel that sense of fulfillment.

- **Will you be given a second chance?**

  Finally, you should also know whether or not your superiors will give you a second chance in case your idea fails. As much as you would like to succeed in everything that you do, this won't always be the case. This is why you must prove your worth as an intrapreneur in your organization first. That way, your employers will feel more confident in allowing you to start over.

If you are given this second chance, failure won't seem like the end of the world for you. In fact, the lessons you learn from your failure will also give you some other kind of fulfillment since you know that you can do better the next time around.

Chapter 5:

Failure is a Part of Success

It's time to stop thinking of failure as the end of the line. The most successful intrapreneurs know in their hearts that failure is part of success. But the reality is that most people are afraid to fail, and this is one of the reasons why they don't even want to try. If you want to be successful in your endeavors, you must embrace failures and see them as learning experiences.

When you see successful people, don't think that they got where they are without failing once or twice in their lives. All of these people had experienced failure, but they didn't let this stop them. They picked themselves up, learned from their experience, and kept on trying until they finally achieved what they had set out to do. And this is what you must do as well if you want to become a successful intrapreneur.

The Importance of Failure

Failure is an important part of life. If you dream of becoming a huge success and achieving all of your goals, you must take this aspect into consideration as well. Failure isn't something you must avoid at all costs. When it happens (and it will), accept it and move on. Here are some reasons why failure is an important part of success as well as your journey towards intrapreneurship:

- **It makes you stronger**

  Although some people see failure as something that brings them down, it also has the potential to build you up and make you stronger. Of course, this only happens when you keep going even after you fail. If you manage to overcome your failures, you emerge as a stronger and wiser person who's ready to take on more challenging situations.

- **It gives you a sense of direction**

  People who have never failed in their lives tend to second guess all of the decisions they make. When this happens, they don't really know the direction they should be taking on the road to success. As an intrapreneur, you must have a clear sense of direction. Remember that you will be helping your company grow and succeed. If you fail, you will get a better idea of where you should go. So, don't feel discouraged when you fail. Instead, use this opportunity to find the right path.

- **It teaches you new things**

  When you fail, you learn why it happened. You learn where you went wrong, and you learn more about your weaknesses. No matter how confident you were when you started on a plan or a project, failure will always be there to teach you new things. Also, failure will keep you grounded. Success has the tendency to get into our heads easily. But when you fail, you learn how to value what's really important in order to succeed.

- **It helps you overcome your fears**

  As previously mentioned, a lot of people won't even bother trying because they're afraid of failure. Even if they're afraid of other things, failure is always more overpowering. But if you change how you see failure, if you stop looking at it as something negative, this will help you overcome your fears more easily. Then you can start taking more risks and working out of your comfort zone to become a better and more efficient member of your organization.

- **It's a valuable opportunity**

  Rather than thinking of all the negative things associated with failure, why not focus on this being a valuable opportunity to learn something new and to prove your worth? Failing teaches you to persist and to be resilient even though the odds are stacked against you. When you're able to succeed after you've failed, this shows you and those around you how mentally capable and strong you are. So, you should start seeing failure as an opportunity to make yourself better by correcting your mistakes.

How to Make Your Failures Part of Your Success

Failure doesn't always have to be a problem. Sure, it may cause delays and some negative feelings, but it also has the potential to make you a better person in the long run. Intrapreneurs don't allow failures to defeat them. They don't allow their failures to make them feel like they won't ever achieve anything in their lives ever again. So, if you want to make your failures part of your success, here are some tips for you:

- **Change the way you define failure**

  This is the first thing you must do if you want to learn from your failures instead of losing to them. Although this is easier said than done, it's entirely possible. Think of failure as something positive, something you can learn from and the next time you experience it, you won't feel as bad. Of course, changing your definition of failure won't make failing feel less painful. Accept these negative feelings, allow yourself to grieve for some time then move on. The more you do this, the easier it becomes for you to accept the new definition of failure you've thought of.

- **Don't think that things will automatically be better next time**

  After you've failed at a certain endeavor, don't assume that the next time you try, things will automatically be better. Although this may happen sometimes, this isn't always the case. Remember that there are countless ways a certain situation may play out. So, even if you planned more carefully the next time around, you might still fail. This is a very real possibility you have to accept and deal with. Each time you fail, make adjustments to your strategy until you finally experience the success.

- **Break down your failure to find out what went wrong**

  Remember how you can learn new things from failure? The best way to do this is to break down the situation and analyze it, so you can find out exactly what went wrong. If you have the time to do this, then you may be able to achieve success quicker. Breaking down your failure allows you to learn more efficiently from it.

- **Take responsibility for your own failures**

  When you fail, accept it and take responsibility for it. Intrapreneurs are always trying to find ways to make things better. So, if you made a plan and it failed, don't point fingers at other people just to take the heat off yourself. When you take responsibility for your failures, this makes you a stronger person as well. Those around you will learn to respect you because you don't shy away from challenges nor do you place blame on other people when things don't go your way.

- **Other tips to keep in mind**
    - When you or the people around you make mistakes, this doesn't have to be a problem. Instead, see these as learning opportunities to help you improve.
    - When talking about failure, choose your words carefully. Whether you're trying to talk to yourself or to other people about how you failed and how you can make things better, you must make sure that what you say has a positive impact.
    - It's better to have tried and failed than not to have tried at all just because you were afraid of failure. When you don't do anything, it means you're not learning and you're not striving.
    - Don't let your failure define you. Instead, let it become an important lesson to learn from in order to make you more prepared for the future.

Chapter 6:

Tackle Your Weaknesses?

Part of being an intrapreneur is also learning to accept your weaknesses. Just like your failures, your weaknesses don't have to be a negative thing. Remember that nobody is perfect. No matter how perfect other people may seem, they also have their own weaknesses that they work through.

Often, people try to hide their weaknesses to show others how strong they are. But when you do this, you're just hurting yourself. Instead of hiding, why don't you try working on your weaknesses to turn them into strengths? Doing this is both beneficial and empowering so you may want to start doing this:

Accepting Your Weaknesses

When it comes to your weaknesses, the first thing you must do is learn to accept them. Your weaknesses are part of who you are, and you don't have to be ashamed of them. Just like the times when you fail, learning to accept your weaknesses turns them into something positive. Then you can see them as opportunities to make yourself better.

Most people only focus on their strengths. They focus on improving these qualities as much as they can in order to be the best at what they do. However, it's very rare to encounter people who focus more on their weaknesses and try to turn these into strengths as well. Most of the time, people try to bury their weaknesses and imperfections, so they don't have to worry about them when they're trying to work.

But if you really want to improve yourself, part of the process is improving those things you're not really good at. Accept these imperfections, analyze them, and try to find ways to make them better. Imagine how great you will become if you learn how to master your strengths and improve your weaknesses as well! In doing this, you will also be pushing yourself to reach your fullest potential.

As an intrapreneur, you must also learn not to be too hard on yourself all the time. Yes, you want to be the best version of yourself. But this doesn't mean that you should put yourself down just because you have weaknesses. You can still become a successful intrapreneur even if you have a few imperfections and weaknesses. But when others see how you accept them and not make them a hindrance to your success, they will see you more as an inspiration.

Also, accepting your weaknesses makes you more of a human being. So, as part of your journey, it's time to take a look at your weaknesses so you can start accepting them, understanding them, and working hard to transform them into better things.

Don't Let Your Weaknesses Hold You Back

If you lived in a perfect world, you won't have to deal with weaknesses and imperfections. You can be a strong, successful person who lives a perfect professional and personal life. Sadly though, none of us live in a perfect world. And when you think about it, if life didn't come with challenges, would we really feel happy or fulfilled?

You must learn to accept that you are amazing at some things, but you aren't able to do others. For the latter, these are known as your weaknesses. Although having these weaknesses can be extremely frustrating at times, you don't have to let them hold you back from becoming an amazing intrapreneur or an amazing person. Here are some pointers to guide you if you want to transform your weaknesses into strengths:

- **Accept your weaknesses**

  We've already discussed this in the previous section but it's definitely worth mentioning again. The first thing you must do is accept that you have weaknesses, so that you can start improving them. If you have to, make a list of these weaknesses and arrange them according to which ones you want to work on first.

- **Ask help from someone whom you trust**

When you try to improve your weaknesses, this can make you feel vulnerable, especially at the beginning. One thing you can do to cope with such a situation is to ask help from someone whom you trust. Make sure to choose this person wisely.

The person you choose must have a genuine concern for you and must want to see you succeed. Such a person can help you focus on improving your weaknesses and provide you with moral support whenever you feel like the situation has taken a turn for the worst.

- **Prepare yourself**
If you know that you're about to perform a task which requires a skill you're not really good at, the best thing you can do is prepare for it. This is another excellent way to keep moving forward despite your weaknesses. For instance, if you have a presentation and you're not really good at speaking in front of people (which, by the way, is a skill that can be improved through practice), then make sure your presentation compensates for your weakness.

Come up with an incredible and memorable presentation which will catch the attention of your audiences. Using different kinds of relevant media may distract your audience from the fact that you're not that great at speaking in front of them. Of course, you should also try to improve on this skill every chance you get!

- **Hire professionals to help you out**

  In some cases, you don't even have time to work on your weaknesses. You may be given a task, which you know you cannot do on your own and you have a deadline to meet. In such a case, you may hire a professional to help you out at least for this one task. This means that you would have to pay for the services of a professional, but you will also learn from what they do. While you work with professionals, ask for some advice or tips, which may help you turn your weakness into something you're good at.

- **Aim for adequacy**

  This may seem like odd advice for intrapreneurship, but it perfectly applies to weaknesses. Instead of making yourself feel bad that you can't perfect something you're really bad at, you may want to aim for adequacy. As long as you're "good enough" at the thing you used to be really bad at, you would have already successfully turned this weakness into something better.

- **Look for other people who share the same weaknesses and work together to improve**

  Finally, you can also ask around to find out if there are any other people in your workplace who share the same weaknesses as you. Working together with such people may keep you motivated. Also, you can learn new strategies from each other as you work together to improve yourselves.

PART 2:
WHERE YOU ARE

Chapter 7:

Know Where You're Working Now

The next thing to think about on your intrapreneurship journey is the kind of company you work in right now. There are so many kinds of companies out there and you will seldom find two companies which are identical to each other. But one thing they have in common is that they have their own incredible intrapreneurs and intrapreneurs in the making and these people are the ones who make the company great. Here are some of the kinds of industries you may start your career in:

1. **Banking, Finance, and Accountancy**

   When you work in this industry, you must be very comfortable with numbers. You must be extremely organized, have a great eye for detail, and you must also possess professional qualifications. As an intrapreneur in this industry, you may want to search for ways to make processes faster and more efficient for the benefit of your clients and of the company.

2. Business and Management

This is one of the more popular industries in the world now which means that employees for companies in this industry are in high demand. If you're able to contribute to the success of a company in this industry, you're sure to become a valuable asset. Just make sure that you're able to work in a fast-paced environment and you're highly adaptable which, coincidentally, is an important trait of intrapreneurs!

3. Construction

Although working in this type of industry doesn't always involve manual labor, you should prepare yourself to do a lot of hands-on work. But even in such a work environment, you can still become an intrapreneur by trying to learn new ways to make work easier, finding suppliers to save on material costs, and so much more.

4. Creative Arts

When it comes to creative arts, there are so many different kinds of jobs to choose from. And the best part about working in this industry is that you can use your own creativity to improve yourself and your company.

5. Environmental Care

This industry works best for those who love nature and the outdoors. We now live in a world where we are becoming more conscious of the importance of preserving our resources and the environment. Therefore, there are also a lot of opportunities for you to become an intrapreneur in this kind of work environment.

6. Manufacturing and Engineering

This industry is quite popular too, especially since technology is gradually taking over the world. So, if you plan to work in a company which is all about manufacturing and engineering, prepare to come up with a lot of ideas to pitch to your bosses for the overall improvement of the company.

7. Marketing, Media, and Advertising

These industries are a lot like the creative arts industries. You need to have enough knowledge about the workings of the companies in these industries in order to succeed in them. As you learn more about the job you hold, you may also want to start learning how to become an intrapreneur in this type of working environment too. Since these industries are very broad in nature, finding ways to contribute and improve them won't be much of a challenge.

8. Sales and Retail

For this industry, you must be a real people person.

Companies in sales and retail are focused on their clients and customers, so you may want to keep this in mind when you're thinking of intrapreneurial strategies. As long as the change you plan to suggest is beneficial to the customers and the company, there's a high chance of getting good feedback.

As you can see, there are many different types of industries you can work in and there are different ways for you to become a successful intrapreneur in these industries. You should know where you want to work and where you think you can excel in. Other industries you might be interested are:

- Healthcare
- Hospitality
- Information Technology
- Law
- Leisure and Sports
- Public Services and Office Administration
- Research and Science
- Security
- Social Work
- Teaching and Education

Different Types of Environments to Work in

Apart from the different kinds of industries you can work in, each company provides different types of work environments for their employees. As an intrapreneur, you must know about these environments in order to come up with the proper strategies to achieve your goals and the objectives of the company as well. Here are some of the most common examples of work environments you may find and experience:

- **Open skeptic environment**

  In this type of environment, you are encouraged to question everything before you are encouraged to ask questions. Therefore, if you plan to suggest a new plan for a marketing strategy, you may have to explain first why this plan of yours is better than the one which already exists. Here, you won't be reprimanded or judged because of your ideas as long as you're able to defend these well.

- **Individual-focused environment**

  Here, individuals are allowed to be flexible in terms of their working styles. You may even opt to work from home as long as this doesn't interfere with your productivity. Flexible working hours are also common for this type of environment thus, employees work in different ways.

- **No-walls environment**

  Companies which promote this type of environment are focused on keeping all of the members of their team together. You won't find cubicles or offices which separate the employees from each other, and employees can freely communicate with one another.

- **Mutual-feedback environment**

  Here, you are encouraged to give your honest feedback whenever there is a need for it. Such an environment places great importance on improvement and employees must trust each other to provide, listen to, and apply mutual feedback.

- **Unified environment**

  In this type of environment, employees are encouraged to work individually but are also encouraged to focus on the success of their team. Usually, employers would set goals for the whole team then assign the employees to work in smaller groups or to work individually on tasks to achieve the main goal. This type of environment encourages accountability.

- **Star-studded environment**

  Companies which offer this type of environment hire individuals who are hard-driving and fiercely competitive. They have their own personal goals and they tend to compare their own success against others as they want to be the best in the organization. Working in such a company can be extremely challenging, especially if you're not the competitive type.

- **Cause-driven environment**

  In this environment, you may encounter a lot of servant leaders. Employees don't worry as much about their personal triumphs or individual happiness. Rather, they are more focused on helping others and going the extra mile to meet the needs of their coworkers, clients, employers, and even their community.

- **Intimate environment**

  There are also intimate environments wherein the employees who work together know each other well. Usually, you would see this type of work environment in smaller companies, which don't have a lot of employees.

Although these are the most common types of environments you can work in, there are others which exist as well. The important thing is to know what you're good at and this may help you determine the best type of environment where you can grow and flourish as an intrapreneur.

Chapter 8:

Becoming a Better You, No Matter Where You Are

Now that you know more about where you are right now, this information should help you come up with a strategy for your self-improvement. No matter where you are in your career, what type of industry you've chosen to work in, and what type of environment you're currently employed in, you must learn how to enhance yourself if you want to become an intrapreneur.

Intrapreneurship isn't a new concept. It has been around for some time now and people have been transforming themselves into intrapreneurs since they learned how to do it. If you also want to become one of these successful intrapreneurs in the workplace, you must learn how to do this right now. There's no time like the present and it doesn't matter where you are! As long as you start running things and pushing yourself to reach your full potential, you are already on your way to becoming a true intrapreneur.

Accept the Environment You're In

Acceptance is one thing that you will keep on encountering on your journey to becoming an intrapreneur. Before you can start improving your skills and yourself, you must accept the environment you're in right now. Keep in mind that intrapreneurs aim to succeed as they help their company grow and succeed as well. But how can you do this if you don't accept where you are right now?

If you're not happy with your work, you're not alone. As a matter of fact, most people aren't really happy with their jobs nor are they happy with the environment where they work. But if you want to become an intrapreneur within your company, you must let go of this mindset and start learning how to accept your current situation.

If the acceptance doesn't come right away, don't worry about it. Learning how to become an intrapreneur is a process which may even help you feel happier and more satisfied with your job. As you learn to accept your environment, you will be able to start exercising your creativity, building your credibility, and making a more meaningful impact on your company. This is the essence of being an intrapreneur and it starts with acceptance.

Work on Improving Yourself No Matter Where You Are

After accepting your work environment, it's time to start improving yourself. When you're able to let go of all the negative feelings you have about your company, you will start having a genuine concern for it. You will start learning how you can become a great intrapreneur who has the potential to make a difference in the company. To help you out with these, here are some points to think about:

- **Build an intrapreneurial culture**
  This doesn't mean that you have to "create" intrapreneurs as you're also learning how to be one. Even though such people aren't aware that they have the potential to be intrapreneurs within the organization, chances are, they already exist. So, all you have to do is to discover them, nurture them, and encourage them to be great intrapreneurs as well.

- **Be inclusive**
  Just because you don't see the qualities of intrapreneurs in other people, this doesn't mean that you should shun them. Each and every person in the organization matters no matter how small the job they hold is. As you work to improve yourself and your company, include others in your journey to make it more meaningful.

- **Give ownership to others**
  Even as an intrapreneur, you don't have to make all the decisions in the company. Empower others by allowing them to make decisions and to take ownership over

those decisions that they make. This shows others that you respect them no matter how much you have grown and contributed to the organization.

- **Be okay with risk-taking**
  Risk-taking is another concept which you will keep on encountering as an intrapreneur. Before you take risks, you must learn how to analyze the situation first. If you just keep taking risks without thinking, you might end up having a reputation in the office for being impulsive and taking actions without thinking. The key is to take calculated risks which have a higher chance of success than those risks you take for the sake of being called a risk-taker.

- **Learn how to be comfortable with your own self**
  Finally, you must learn how to be comfortable with your own self. Now that you have accepted your environment and you're ready for self-improvement, it's time for you to release all of those doubts and negative emotions. This will help unleash your potential even more as you move forward in your endeavor.

Chapter 9:

Never Settle!

You should never settle for things that don't benefit you. Sure, you receive a salary regularly, but you shouldn't settle for just this. You should aim to contribute, succeed, and create an environment which promotes you. If what you're doing now doesn't make you feel fulfilled and you know that you can do more, then make changes in your life!

Time is a valuable resource and there's no point wasting it on things that don't make you feel satisfied, happy or content. If you want to become an intrapreneur but you have too many fixed expenses and no savings, it's time to make a change.

If You're Not Happy, Leave!

You can only become a true intrapreneur within your organization if you're happy where you are. If you feel angry, bitter, resentful or you're feeling any other negative emotions towards your employer, the people you work with or your working environment, then you would find it extremely difficult to learn how to improve yourself and the company you're working in.

So, if you're not happy, leave!

Unfortunately, a lot of people choose to stay where they are even though they're feeling miserable each and every day. But why do that to yourself? Why would you stick with a job that you hate, and doesn't make you feel fulfilled? There's really no reason for you to do this to yourself.

Instead of wallowing in your misery, pick yourself up, apply the intrapreneurial strategies you've learned so far to your own life, and start looking for a company that will make you happier and will motivate you to become the best intrapreneur you can be! When you're trying to search for the best organization or company where you can start your intrapreneurial journey, consider the following:

- **The people**

  Consider the team you will be working with. Ask about the average age of the members of the team. Does it seem like you can start building strong relationships with those people? If the answer to this last question is yes, then you should definitely join that team or organization.

- **The growth and development opportunities**

  As an intrapreneur, you should also look into the opportunities for professional growth and development.

This is important, especially if you want to move forward in your career whether vertically or horizontally.

- **The type of work**

  If you're not happy with your work now, you might want to apply for a different type of work; one that will make you feel more content and fulfilled at the end of the day. You've already assessed your best skills and your weaknesses. So, now it's time to look for a job where you know you'll do great.

- **The compensation**

  Although you won't be measuring your success as an intrapreneur by the money you earn, you must still be realistic. If you have a lot of expenses, then you must find a job that will allow you to sustain your current way of life while still being able to set aside some money for a rainy day.

  Just because you want to become a valuable asset of the company, this doesn't mean that you should settle for a job that won't pay you enough. Then you'd be worrying more about how you'll pay for everything instead of being able to focus on your intrapreneurial journey.

- **Other factors**

  Think about the other factors that would make you a

happier member of the organization. Some of these factors include the commute, the exit opportunities offered by the company, whether or not you will feel motivated with the work you'll be doing, and so on.

The bottom line is that if you want to change jobs because you're not happy where you are right now, then you should find one you're sure will make you feel happier and more motivated.

Being Content While Striving for More

Of course, even if you are happy and content with where you are and what you do right now, this doesn't mean that you shouldn't strive for more. You must keep pushing yourself to become better, be more innovative, and be a more courageous member of the team. If you're thinking about ways which can help you strive for more even though you already feel content, here are some suggestions:

- **Strengthen your credibility**

  Whether you've just started a new job or you've been working in the company but you've chosen to start your intrapreneurship journey, you must start building and strengthening your credibility. This means that when you say anything to others, you must do it. Whether you've offered to help another person or you told someone that you'll come up with a plan to make things better, you should follow through.

The more credible you are, the more people will believe you and the more motivated they will feel by your actions. Conversely, if you keep making big plans or you keep bragging about how much you've helped others in the past, but they never see you actually lift a finger, this would hurt your credibility. If you want to become an intrapreneur in your organization, credibility is extremely important, so you should strive for this.

- **Search for an unmet need**

  Although you may be content with your job right now, this doesn't mean that the organization is perfect. This is where you come in as an intrapreneur. Do research on your own company and try to find out if there is an unmet need or overlooked issue that you can start working on. Even if the issue doesn't directly affect you, it's still possible for you to think of ways to solve it to make things better for your workplace.

- **Create heroes**

  As an intrapreneur, you should also be in the business of creating heroes. Strive to do things which will make your team the hero of the organization or you can work with other intrapreneurs you work with to make your whole organization a hero in your community. This would entail a lot of planning and work but, the rewards are definitely worth it.

- **Don't wait around for people to tell you what to do**

  Finally, striving means that you don't wait around for other people to tell you what to do. Intrapreneurs never sit back contentedly while twiddling their thumbs until the next task comes along. Remember that you must have the initiative to find work that will make you more productive and will help your company grow and move forward.

PART 3:
WHO ARE THE PEOPLE AROUND YOU

Chapter 10:

Dealing with People in Power

As an intrapreneur, you must learn how to deal with different types of people. Start from the top and work your way down. It's important for you to learn how to deal with your superiors such as managers, executives, directors, and other people above you. You must work with them and let them understand how you plan to help your organization grow.

The people who hold the power in your organization must learn how to deal with and nurture your intrapreneurial personality to help you improve and share what you have to offer. Even if you're not close to your boss or you don't particularly like them, you must remember that you work for them. Therefore, you should never lose your respect for those in power (or for anyone else in the organization for that matter) as they might show you the same courtesy. Here are some of the most basic tips to keep in mind when dealing with people in power:

- **Remember that your superiors are human beings too**

  Yes, they hold the power, but you must remember that they are human too. Your boss doesn't have the ability to read your mind, so if you want to do something for the betterment of your organization, tell them about it. Also, try to understand why your boss might reject some of your ideas, especially when you haven't proven your worth yet. Be patient and keep trying. The more you show how well your ideas pan out, the more credible you become. Soon, your boss will trust you enough to take the reins and execute your own plans.

- **Communicate**

  This is one of the most important things you can do when dealing with people in power. There's no need to hide anything from your boss if you're not doing anything wrong. No matter what you want to say, be open with your boss about it. Communication is key and you must learn how to manage this well if you want to be respected and accepted as an intrapreneur.

Never Forget Your Professionalism

If you want to succeed as an intrapreneur, you must try to build a strong relationship with your boss. After all, you do work for the organization. If you want to be the one running things, then you'd be better off becoming an entrepreneur. One of the most important things to keep in mind if you want to maintain a good relationship with those in power is to never forget your professionalism. No matter how much you may disagree with your boss or how much you want to fight for what you believe in, never throw your professionalism out the door. Here's some things to keep in mind:

- **Learn how to empathize**
  There will be times when you will feel negatively towards your boss, this is normal. But in times like these, instead of picking a fight with your boss, try empathizing with them. There is always a reason for how your boss acts, so try putting yourself in their shoes. No matter how much pressure you feel at work, remember that your boss is probably feeling double that pressure. So, don't be too hard on your boss. This will help you minimize those negative feelings.

- **Try to make your boss look good**
  What boss wouldn't love looking good because their subordinates are working beyond expectation? One of the ways you can get on your boss' good side is to do your work so well that your whole team gets recognized for it. And when this happens, it will make your boss look good too!

- **Become the brand ambassador of your team**

As much as possible, try to be the "cheerleader" of your team. Keep reminding everyone about the importance of your team and why each of you should be doing your best at all times. The more you help your team grow, the more your boss will notice your efforts. Soon, your boss may see you as more of a leader or an ambassador who keeps things running smoothly.

- **Be a mentor to your boss**

  This point can be quite tricky, but it will also pay off in the end. If you know that your boss is struggling with some tasks or you possess skills, which you know your boss can benefit from learning, you can respectfully offer your help. If your boss is also interested in self-improvement, he will appreciate this gesture. Of course, if you know your boss doesn't appreciate this kind of help, then you might have to approach the situation in a different way.

How to Deal with People in Power as an Intrapreneur

Now that you know more about how you can "manage" your boss, it's time to start thinking like an intrapreneur. You don't have to manipulate your boss just to get what you want or just so you can move forward in your career. As long as you work genuinely and you do your best, these actions will speak for themselves. As an intrapreneur, the best way you can deal with your bosses and get on their good sides is by employing a number of effective skills and smart habits.

First of all, you should always aim to solve problems and not create them. Problems will always be part of any organization and you should avoid being the cause of it. In fact, one of the easiest ways to solve a problem is to stop being a part of it. Step back and try to look at the problem with a new perspective, then you can start thinking of ways to solve the problem. Go through the solutions you've thought of, eliminate those that might not be too feasible, then approach your boss with these solutions.

Another thing you can do is to try and remain calm no matter how chaotic your environment becomes. When things start to fall apart, you shouldn't lose your cool nor should you start panicking with the rest of them. Show your superiors that you can handle pressure and you can focus on the more important things no matter how bad things may get.

Also, take responsibility for your own actions. If your boss confronts you with an issue that you might have caused (even indirectly), accept your mistake as well as the consequences that might come with it. Then offer to find a solution to the problem, especially since you're the reason it happened in the first place. People respect those who hold themselves accountable instead of blaming others for the wrong things they did.

Finally, you should also set boundaries and follow them. Although you want to build a strong relationship with your boss, remember that you aren't at the same level. So, no matter how well you get along, always maintain your professionalism and give respect where it is due. That way, your boss knows that you respect boundaries and they, in turn, will learn to respect you too.

Chapter 11:

Dealing with Your Coworkers

Employees within organizations are easy to intimidate, especially those who aren't happy with where they are and what they're doing. Although you work with such coworkers, you should still learn how to deal with them in the best possible way. As an intrapreneur, you should learn how to motivate your coworkers and inspire them to do better through your much-deserved progress and success.

This is one of the hardest things you would have to do as an intrapreneur but it's also extremely rewarding. When you see how you have made a positive impact on the productivity of your coworkers, this will definitely make you feel more fulfilled. Never give up on your journey and never give up on your coworkers either. The more they see how much you want them to succeed, the more likely they are to start pushing themselves to do better as well.

Appreciating Your Differences

When you work in an organization, you have to accept the fact that your coworkers are different from you. It's highly unlikely to land a job where all the employees are trying to become intrapreneurs. Even if you do end up in such a company, you would still have to deal with the different personalities and goals of the people you work with. The best way to do this is by appreciating other people's differences.

Just because you're different from your coworkers - in this case, you aim to become an intrapreneur but they're perfectly fine just being employees - that doesn't mean that you can't work together. Here are some ways to deal with your coworkers:

- **Don't take things personally**

  Unless you've really done something to make others feel bad, there's really no reason for your coworkers to personally attack you or to not show warmth towards you. Try to look at the situation before you feel bad or react in a certain way. If your coworkers don't warm up to you right away or they don't show the same level of enthusiasm as you, this doesn't mean that they don't like you as a person. They have their own reasons for acting the way they do, which doesn't really relate to you.

- **Consider their feelings**

  When you pitch an idea and it's not received as well as

you thought it would be, try to consider how your coworkers feel about your idea. Maybe it entails more work for them and you're the only one who's willing to put in the extra effort or maybe the idea you suggested went against their beliefs. Speak to your coworkers about how they feel about things and you'll be able to gain insight on how to approach situations in the future.

- **Start conversations with them**
  Just like when you're dealing with people in power, communication is key. If you don't start conversations with your coworkers, how would you know how to deal with them? Whether you want to convince them to get on board or you just want to learn more about them, starting a conversation will be very beneficial for you.

How to Deal with Your Coworkers as an Intrapreneur

As an intrapreneur, you must find ways to deal with your coworkers in order to help them appreciate what you're doing instead of interpreting your actions in a negative way. Remember that there will always be those who won't understand your efforts, especially if they don't like their jobs to begin with. Although such people are more challenging to deal with, just be patient and you'll see your efforts pay off after some time. If not, at least you tried!

But for those coworkers who are easier to get along with and who are more appreciative of intrapreneurs and other helpful people in the workplace, you won't have to try too hard. Either way, here are some strategies you can employ when dealing with different kinds of coworkers:

- **Always encourage teamwork**
  When you're able to work together well, this will make everyone's job easier. Spread your enthusiasm around and encourage collaboration between the members of your team. Encourage them to speak up and when good ideas come, nurture them and work together to make them a reality.

- **Allow others to grow with you and with the company**
  As you try to grow as a professional and as an intrapreneur, allow others to grow with you too. Even though they aren't interested in becoming intrapreneurs, allow your coworkers to grow professionally in the way they want to grow. As long as they're not doing anything wrong, encourage this growth. And as you're all moving forward, the company will also start experiencing growth and success.

- **Share the fundamentals of intrapreneurship**
  You don't have to force your coworkers to become intrapreneurs if they don't want to. But as you know, the fundamental concepts and strategies of intrapreneurship

are great for the company. So, you can try introducing these fundamentals without having to push intrapreneurship on others. Choose the concepts that you believe your coworkers will accept and introduce these in a creative way.

- **Don't trump other people's individuality**
  After you've accepted the individual differences of your coworkers, you should also encourage them to express their individuality. When you do this, you're also helping them reach their fullest potential because you're not trying to hinder them in any way.

- **Teach others not to fear failure**
  Finally, you should also help quell the fears of your coworkers when it comes to failure. Since you've already learned how to make your failures a part of your success, you can share this knowledge, so your coworkers will be braver and will start looking at the positive side of their own failures.

Basically, when it comes to dealing with coworkers, you don't have to change who you are. As long as you learn to accept the differences of others, you will be able to deal with different kinds of people as an intrapreneur.

Chapter 12:

Dealing with Family and Friends

After you've made the choice to become an intrapreneur, you would also have to share this journey with your family and friends. These are the people closest to you and they deserve to know all about intrapreneurship. In fact, some people even talk to their family and friends first *before* they actually begin their change. The timing of when you want to share this choice to your loved ones depends on you. As long as you tell them about your intrapreneurial journey, they can be your support system when you meet challenges along the way.

Sharing Your Knowledge with the People Closest to You

If you love the organization you're working in, the people you work with, and your job and you want to become a better person for them, then becoming an intrapreneur is definitely a step in the right direction. Although intrapreneurship comes with a lot of benefits, it doesn't come with a guarantee that you'll never face difficulties or challenges along the way.

The good news is that you don't have to face this journey on your own. If you want to start off strong and have the right people supporting you throughout your endeavor, then you may want to share this news to the people closest to you. After you've learned about intrapreneurship from different resources such as this book, you can talk to your family and friends about making a change from becoming an employee to becoming an intrapreneur.

Sharing this with the people who know you the best allows you to go into intrapreneurship with more insight from the different perspectives of those around you. Who knows, you may have friends and family members who are already intrapreneurs! This means that they can share their own real-life experiences of how they started, the challenges they faced, and how they overcame those challenges.

Advice from the people you love is always invaluable. Since they know you well, they can be as honest as possible when giving you advice. Of course, you should learn as much as you can about intrapreneurship before you speak to those closest to you. That way, you can answer any questions they may have about it. Think of it like a practice run. If you're able to answer even the most difficult questions, then it means that you have learned enough and you're ready to start becoming an intrapreneur.

Even if they ask you something which you have no answer to, you can look at this as an opportunity to learn more about things you may have overlooked. Either way, speaking to the people closest to you gives you a better idea of how to deal with others too. When the going gets tough, you can rely on your loved ones to encourage and motivate you because you've already given them a heads-up on what to expect! It's definitely a win-win situation.

Chapter 13:

Dealing with Entrepreneurs and Other Intrapreneurs

Whether you're in a professional or social setting, you would have to deal with entrepreneurs and other intrapreneurs alike. As you're learning how to become a true intrapreneur, you must learn how to deal with these types of people, so that you're always on top of the situation.

You don't have to feel intimidated by other intrapreneurs or by entrepreneurs when you meet such people. After all, you've also decided to learn how to be like them. Instead of feeling intimidated, you should strike up a conversation with these people in order to learn from them and share your own insights from the experiences you've had.

Working Hand-in-Hand with Entrepreneurs

We've already gone through the definitions of entrepreneurs and intrapreneurs in the earlier parts of this book. Basically, intrapreneurs are simply entrepreneurs who work within a bigger company or organization. So, at the very core, you're really not that different from an entrepreneur. The main difference you have is that an entrepreneur has made the choice to start their own organization. So, your boss may be an entrepreneur!

When it comes to dealing with entrepreneurs, you don't have to see them as "the competition." You share the same basic beliefs, values, and principles so it's better for you to work with them instead of challenging them. Let's take a look at some pointers you can do to help you work hand-in-hand with entrepreneurs inside or outside of your organization:

- **Don't be shy**

  Just because you haven't made the choice to start your own business, this doesn't mean that you should feel shy that you've chosen to "just become an intrapreneur." This choice takes great courage as it will force you to move out of your comfort zone. So, if you meet an entrepreneur, don't be afraid to talk to them and share what you have learned as well.

- **Offer help without being pushy**

  Entrepreneurs need help too. They don't have everything figured out, so you may want to offer to help. Just don't be too over eager or pushy as this might be interpreted in a negative way. Make suggestions, offer solutions, and even give advice when you feel like it's needed. If done properly, your efforts will be highly appreciated.

- **Advertise your own organization**

  Remember that as an intrapreneur, you're genuinely interested in helping your company succeed. So, you must always be the brand ambassador of your organization. When meeting entrepreneurs outside of your organization, talk about how incredible your own organization is. You never know, these entrepreneurs you meet may be looking for partners or suppliers and your company may be just what they're looking for. The more you talk about the things that make your company great, the more you will attract other entrepreneurs to patronize your business.

Sharing Common Ground with Other Intrapreneurs

Although there are no organizations lucky enough to have 100% intrapreneurs working for them, you may still encounter an intrapreneur or two within your own organization. This is a great thing for you because you can help each other learn, grow, and improve. When you meet other intrapreneurs in your company, you share common ground with them. You must also learn how to deal with such people well, so you don't create conflicts with like-minded people. Here are some tips for you:

1. **Find the intrapreneurs in your organization**

   Of course, this is the first thing you must do if you want to discover who are the other intrapreneurs you work with. Keep in mind that intrapreneurs have specific traits that make them stand out from the rest. When looking for intrapreneurs, look for people who:

   a. Increase your organization's productivity.
   b. Try to solve problems even without being told.
   c. Have a lot of innovative plans and ideas.
   d. Take calculated risks and aren't afraid of failure.

2. **Communicate with them**

   Once you've identified the intrapreneurs in your organization, it's time to start communicating with them. Learn more about these people, why they chose to become intrapreneurs, what they've learned throughout their journey, how you can help each other, and other things you want to learn.

3. **Empower each other**

   As you learn more about the other intrapreneurs you work with, you may also want to find ways to empower each other. One of the best ways to do this is by helping each other overcome your weaknesses. If you discover that these other intrapreneurs have skills that you consider your weaknesses, then you can ask them to help you improve and vice versa.

4. Be transparent

There's nothing worse than finding out that people try to get to know you just because they have an ulterior motive in mind. Show your co-intrapreneurs enough respect to be as transparent as possible with them. Be honest with your intentions to show them how genuine you are.

5. Encourage healthy competition and collaboration

Part of working with intrapreneurs is having a healthy kind of competition with them. This kind of competition benefits the company in a great way because you all try to work towards a single goal without having ill feelings towards each other. When you're not competing, you should collaborate with the other intrapreneurs in your organization to come up with better, more innovative ideas for the benefit of everyone.

PART 4:
WHO WILL YOU BECOME

Chapter 14:

You're Part of the Next Generation

Knowing more about yourself is an important step in becoming an intrapreneur. In the past chapters, we've talked about who you are, where you are, and who are the people around you. If you paired your reading with self-reflection and consideration, then you would have a better idea of how you plan to attack this big change you want to make in your life.

Now it's time to think about the future. Although you now work in a company and you're learning how to become an intrapreneur, you have the potential to be the part of the next generation of entrepreneurs, Presidents, Executives, and CEOs of companies in the future. All the efforts you put into your career now will take you to the place where you want to be, where you strive to be.

What are Your Doing Right Now for Your Future?

Being an intrapreneur means that you make it your responsibility to help your company grow and succeed. Of course, this doesn't mean that you shouldn't plan for your own success as well. When you just focus on your company, you might not be left with anything for yourself in the future. You must also focus on your own growth and success. After all, if you don't improve yourself, how can you possibly improve others around you or the organization you work in, right?

An intrapreneur is a person who works as an entrepreneur within a bigger organization. As an intrapreneur, you are a vital part of your organization's continued innovation. As you help others improve, you are also improving because you're learning a lot of things along the way. Throughout this journey, the things you should be doing must contribute to the brightness of your future. Here are some quick tips for you as you're thinking about what you're doing right now for your future:

- Harness your desire to grow, improve, and succeed in the future.
- Reflect on what you can invest willingly.
- Create a team of employees and intrapreneurs who can help you on your journey towards greatness.
- Come up with long-term plans and strategies, which will help your company as well as yourself.
- If you want to become an intrapreneur, just do it already!

Be an Inspiration to Others

This is another way for you to prepare yourself for the future. Learn how to become an inspiration to others instead of just pushing people to do what you want. If you want to become an intrapreneur now but something more in the future, then you should learn how to inspire other people.

If you want to become a better person in the future, you must stop making excuses now. It's easy to make excuses but it's difficult to start taking responsibility. Even when you want to start your intrapreneurship journey, you can keep coming up with excuses to delay this. Then one day you'll wake up and realize that so much time has passed that you have forgotten what you've learned about intrapreneurship. Excuses are for those who want to take the easy route, not for those who want to succeed.

Start working with others, really working with them. This doesn't just mean that you do your own thing while your coworkers do their own thing as well. Collaboration is an important part of any company and it's an important part of intrapreneurship as well. Whether you work with your superiors, your coworkers, entrepreneurs or other intrapreneurs, collaboration always makes things better.

You may also want to start thinking like a boss. Place your coworkers and your organization under your wing, so you can start taking responsibility. If you make yourself responsible for where you work and who you work with, you tend to step up your game even more, which helps you out in the long run. Find the courage within yourself to become a true intrapreneur. In doing this, you can help your organization grow while you set yourself up for a better future.

Chapter 15:

Broaden Your Horizons

The main job you choose to have is only a part of what you can do with your life. While you're transforming yourself in your company, you may also want to explore different types of passive incomes or "side hustles", so your money will start working for you. Since you're basically an entrepreneur within an organization, learning how to earn passive income is important.

Although the term "intrapreneur" did not exist in the past, such people were already working within their own companies. It's just that they weren't labeled as such. They were simply seen as amazing employees who worked hard and helped uplift their organizations.

Needless to say, even though you plan to become an intrapreneur, this doesn't mean that you can't broaden your horizons. The more you improve yourself, the more opportunities you will have to grow and succeed in things you didn't even see as part of your future!

Make the Most Out of Being an Intrapreneur

No matter where you are, you have the potential to be great and to make a huge impact, and the best way to do this is to become an intrapreneur. It's time to stop living each day in mediocrity. Now is the best time for you to start your journey towards becoming an intrapreneur.

As an intrapreneur, you can make a significant change within your organization to help yourself, others, and your company reach their goals. When you leverage your intrapreneurial behaviors, you can create ripples where you can make your workplace more than just a place where you work. To make the most out of being an intrapreneur, you must think innovatively and combine this with risk tolerance as well as creative problem-solving each time you're faced with business challenges.

Simply existing as an employee isn't enough. There's no time like the present to start applying what you've learned to your life so you can begin to see the incredible changes intrapreneurship can bring to your life both professionally and personally.

Learn Ways to Earn Passive Income

Before we conclude this book, let's have one bonus topic to help you out even further. Remember how we mentioned "passive income?" This type of income refers to money that you earn without having to put in the effort for it.

Sounds great, right?

Of course, nothing in the world is this simple. If you want to start earning passive income to make your future as an intrapreneur brighter, don't expect to be totally passive, especially at the beginning. There are ways for you to earn money that will allow you to keep your "day job" or the job where you will focus on becoming an intrapreneur.

When it comes to passive income, there are plenty of options. It's important to learn about these options so you can determine which type of passive income would suit you best. After making a choice, you can set it up and keep an eye on it for a period of time to see if it's viable. If the option you've chosen takes off, only then can you enjoy the fruits of your labor. Here are some examples of passive income options you may want to learn more about:

- Invest in Real Estate by purchasing properties or by investing in companies where you can earn through dividend payments.
- If you have extra space, rent it out!
- Download cash-back apps so you can earn while you shop.
- Take a lot of photos and sell them online.
- Create your own website.
- Buy a vending machine or a gumball machine.
- Come up with designs for greeting cards.
- Create your own E-Course.
- De-clutter your life and sell the stuff you don't need

online.

- Create and sell lesson plans.
- Stick ads on your car.
- Create your own YouTube channel and upload a lot of videos.
- Write and publish eBooks.
- Start your own blog.
- Launch your own webinar.
- Try out affiliate marketing.

These are some of the more popular examples of how people are now earning passive income. There are so many resources you can find online to help you learn more about these options. As long as you stick with your choice and you play your cards right, you can start raking in the cash!

Conclusion:

Being the Best Version of Yourself

There you have it, a quick but complete guide to help you become a successful intrapreneur within your own organization. Now that you're armed with knowledge, tips, and strategies, it's time for you to start working on becoming the best possible version of yourself. Nobody will give the skills to you nor will anybody ask you to become a great intrapreneur. This decision lies solely with you.

The good news is that, since you've purchased and read this book, it means that you're interested in learning how to become an intrapreneur. With all the information you've learned from this book, it's time to start prioritizing and strategizing. Make a list of all your best assets and skills then start improving on them. After, make a list of all your weaknesses and find ways to turn them into strengths.

As you learn more about yourself, learn more about your environment and the people around you too. It's all about finding the right balance between improving yourself, your environment, and the people around you. The more you can employ these strategies, the easier it will become for you to shine as an intrapreneur in your organization. As you help yourself improve, you can also start thinking of ways to improve your organization. Work towards achieving your own goals and the goals of your company. In doing this, you will discover how truly great you are and how you can become a true intrapreneur.

Your Thoughts on A Shark in a Fish Tank?

First of all, thank you for purchasing this book. I know you could have picked any number of books to read, but you picked this book and for that I am extremely grateful.

I hope that it added at value and quality to your life. If so, it would be really nice if you could share this book with your friends and family by posting to Facebook and Twitter.

If you enjoyed this book and found some benefit in reading this, I'd like to hear from you and hope that you could take some time to post a review on Amazon. Your feedback and support will help this author to greatly improve his writing craft for future projects and make this book even better.

I wish you all the best in your future success!

Made in the USA
Monee, IL
07 April 2022

94259738R00069